THE
BREXIT
YEARS

A Handbook for Survivors

Published by ATWP
Eastbourne, East Sussex

ISBN 9-780-99344-313-8

Also available as a Kindle ebook
ISBN 9-780-99344-314-5

A catalogue record for this book
is available from the British Library and
the American Library of Congress

Pre-press production
eBook Versions
127 Old Gloucester Street
London WC1N 3AX
www.ebookversions.com

'Diplomacy is one long doctoring of spin. They tried to employ me on it during my time in Government as they steadily shifted the nomenclature of Europe towards the federal goal of a United States of Europe. What was the Common Market became the European Economic Community and then the European Community and now, pending further adjustment, the European Union. So far as I was concerned, these titles were all misnomers.'

Bernard Ingham, The Wages of Spin, (Murray, 2003)

This book is dedicated to those many people, good and bad, and most particularly our children, who have brought us to this point in our lives.

'Wouldst thou know thyself, observe the actions of others, Wouldst thou others know, look thou within thine own heart'

Friedrich Schiller

'

Acknowledgements

We thank those many friends and acquaintances who have helped us in the preparation of this book. Our thanks to Gareth Thomas for helping with IT terms; to Edward Thomas for pointing out a word used in bad taste and for permission to make use of his writings; to Brian Freeland for a telling quotation and for professional guidance; to Scott Montague Murdoch and Ian Robinson for kindly looking over and commenting on various drafts; to Peter Austin for his insights into the way that social media is altering the nature of journalism and 'news'; and to Daniel Evans, Michael and Pauline Black, Tom Hollobone, Jane Hurley, Freya Montague, Cath Pick, Martyn Pick, John Pleydell and Malcolm Webster for other assistance. However, we alone are responsible for any factual errors there may be in these pages and all unattributed expressions of opinion are ours.

Jane Montague
John Pick
Spring 2017

THE
BREXIT
YEARS

A Handbook for Survivors

Jane Montague & John Pick

ATWP

CONTENTS

ARTICLE 50

The Lisbon Treaty 2007

1. Any Member State may decide to withdraw from the Union in accordance with its own constitutional requirements.

2, A Member State which decides to withdraw shall notify the European Council of its intention. In the light of the guidelines provided by the European Commission, the Union shall negotiate and conclude an agreement with that State, setting out the arrangements for its withdrawal, taking account of its future relationship with the Union. That agreement shall be negotiated in accordance with Article 218 (3) of the Treaty, on the functioning of the European Union.

It shall be concluded on behalf of the Union by the Council, acting by a qualified majority, after obtaining the assent of the European Parliament.

3. The treatise shall apply to the state in question from the entry into force of the withdrawal agreement or, failing that for two years after the notification referred to in paragraph 2, *unless the European Council, in agreement with the Member State, agrees to extend this period.*

4. For the purposes of paragraphs 2 and 3 the member of the European Council, or of the Council representing the withdrawing Member State, shall not participate in the discussions of the European Council, or Council or in discussions concerning it.

5. *If a state has withdrawn from the Union and asks to rejoin, its request shall be subject to the procedure referred to in Article 49.*

[*Our Italics*]

1

THE REFERENDUM

Whatever the direction of travel, at least we're now all on the same page.

The Lord Mayor of London

We're by no means out of the woods, economically speaking, and of course challenges remain, but it certainly seems that companies and customers alike are carrying on with business as usual now the referendum is disappearing into the rear view mirror.

Laith Khalaf, Senior Analyst, Hargreaves Lansdown.

Although it was said to be the *most important decision we would make in our lifetimes* and the land reverberated to the sound of independent forecasts of what the 'wrong' result could mean for *hard-working families*, for *investment in the City*, for pensions or *for worker's rights*, rarely, if ever, can a public debate have been conducted in such a mist of tangled metaphor, tacky statistics and witless cant as was the 2016 Referendum. Lost in this impenetrable fug, the plaintive cry of the voters – 'Just give us the facts!' – could scarcely be heard.

Yet what sort of 'facts' could possibly have shed light

on this debate? Indeed, exactly what was it that was being debated? On the face of it, voters were simply being asked whether they were now in favour of 'remaining in' or of 'leaving' the *European Union*? Very well, of what did this Union now consist? There the difficulties began. Casual observers might have been forgiven for thinking that we were already halfway out of it. They might have recalled that a few years previously the UK had refused, with a fastidious shudder, to adopt the Euro as currency. They might also have remembered occasions when UK Prime Ministers, swinging real or metaphorical handbags, had trumpeted forth their delight at the 'concessions' they had wrung from the hard-faced Brussels bureaucrats. And even the youngest voters could hardly be unaware of the fact that quite recently the UK government had refused to accede to the EU's request that it should take its allotted share of the refugees fleeing the battlefields of Syria, Libya and Iraq. Surely we had already positioned ourselves where we wanted to be, relative to this distantly-perceived Union? What was there left to withdraw from? (In this respect it was noteworthy that Google inquiries as to what the EU actually was, peaked on June 24th – the day *after* we had voted to leave it.)

And there was a further problem. The Referendum result, though representing *the will of the people*, had apparently been arrived at in ignorance of the many legal and financial ties which bound us to the EU. It was, we were now told, a mistake to think the country could free itself from the coils of the European Union as easily as somebody could, for example, resign from a social club. Although no other nation had previously left the Union, and although the mechanics of leaving were covered in one short EU statue, the UK's exit would, we gradually learned, inevitably involve long, complicated and costly negotiations. We voters were now being blamed for delivering a verdict which involved years of negotiation before it could be acted upon. *So why had we been asked the question in the first place?*

Had we been asked instead whether the UK should withdraw from the Eurovision Song Contest, the question would have stood a better chance of being understood. Although mention of that popular songfest points up one of the other difficulties facing us in any inquiry involving 'Europe', which is that Europe's borders seem nowadays, to put it mildly, somewhat flexible. Competitors in the 2016 Eurovision Song Contest had, after all, included Israel, Russia – and *Australia*, for heaven's sake.

When the Cabinet Office early in 2016 informed us of the poll date, we knew that a referendum was not a constitutional necessity. There was not the same clamour for one that there had been in 1992 when Mr Major signed the controversial *Maastricht* agreement. In the UK at that time, as in much of mainland Europe, public opinion had been on a knife edge. A referendum in France gave only the narrowest support to the agreement, while in Denmark the vote went against the EU, which decision was only reversed (by means of a second referendum) after the Danes had negotiated a number of exemptions. In the UK however Mr Major, in spite of being under fire from the *Daily Express*, some of the parliamentary opposition and the 'bastards' in his own party, held firm against demands that he consult the people, relying instead on UK Constitutional Precedence which suggested that a Prime Minister, using the Crown Prerogative, could enter into such agreements without holding a public referendum.

However, a referendum was a political necessity for the Tory party. 'We are the only major party offering a European referendum,' Mr Cameron boasted in the run-up to the 2015 election. That was true, although Mr Wilson had held one in 1975, when we voted to join the Common Market and between 2003 and 2008 Mr Blair's New Labour party had come close to promoting another – though with one all-important difference. In the noughties Blair's government had toyed with the idea of holding a referendum on whether the UK should, or should not, join the (then) fourteen other countries as *members of the Euro Zone*. Robin Cook, who was in favour of joining, reminds us of the parameters of the debate:

> The central fallacy of the Eurosceptics is to rail at the limitations on national sovereignty from agreements in Europe. The real limitations on national sovereignty arise from the new realities of the modern world – transnational economic production, the importance of trade as an engine of growth, global threats to our security and environment. The European Union did not create these threats, but is a logical response to them.
>
> The big European test for the [New Labour] government is how it puts some momentum back into the campaign to persuade the British people that it is in their interests to share the same currency as the customers to whom they sell the bulk of their exports.[1]

Not only was the proposed referendum question then quite different, but the two main parties were quite differently aligned. At the 2006 Election New Labour had campaigned to go further in, proposing to *adopt the Euro*. For the Tories

William Hague spoke for the Eurosceptics, touring Britain with a large digital clock telling the voters how many minutes were left to '*Save the Pound*'.

Mr Cameron's motives for promising (and then holding) the 2016 Referendum were above all concerned with the politics of the Tory party. He thought it an opportune time simultaneously to see off the threat from a nascent UKIP and to silence the bastards in his own party. In the Conservative Manifesto for the 2015 election (expecting, his aides told us, to be in coalition once more with the Liberal Democrats) he had promised that when he became Prime Minister, he would hold a referendum on the UK's continuing membership of the EU. But after the Tory Party had gained its modest majority (with the Liberal Democrats almost wiped out) he still went ahead, even though some in his own party feared that the terms of the question – 'would voters wish the UK to remain in, or leave, the EU?' – over-simplified what was at stake.

As if in tacit recognition of this, almost as soon as he'd agreed the question's phrasing Mr Cameron sought to modify its terms. He said the British people would now be asked whether they wished to stay in, or get out of, a *reformed* European Union. But that was another matter entirely! Asking turkeys to vote for Christmas was one thing. Asking them to vote for a *reformed* Christmas would be quite another. The turkeys might reason that a *reformed* Christmas could well be celebrated by general prayer and fasting, or with strictly vegetarian feasts – neither of which would necessarily involve the mass execution of their gobbling companions – and vote accordingly.

This talk of 'reformation' arose from a promise Mr Cameron had made at the 2014 Tory Party Conference. Jaw

jutting, steely-eyed, staring straight into the TV cameras, he pledged:

'Britain, I know you want this sorted, so I will go to Brussels. I will not take 'no' for an answer and – when it comes to free movement – I will get what Britain needs!'

So, before the 2016 hustings got under way, he set out, single handedly, to *sort* it. He flew off on a grand tour of European capitals, aiming at sorting the Union out in a matter of weeks. He was photographed, looking tough and determined, with the leaders of Bulgaria, Albania and the twenty five other EU Presidents and Prime Ministers in whose interests he had, until then, seemed only mildly interested. Moreover he threatened that if they refused to be sorted he would actually campaign to *leave* the EU! But throughout Europe, as well as in the UK, this was assumed to be empty bluster. And when in the end the EU remained unsorted and he was forced to take 'no' for an answer, a deflated Mr Cameron was forced to admit he was, after all, going to campaign to 'remain'. But then his failure to *sort out* the EU cleverly became a reason for voting to remain in it. He and his allies now argued that the UK would need to retain *a seat at the table* in order to *reform* a body in whose *unreformed* clutches he was urging us to remain… or something like that.

Once this convoluted political posture was decided upon, Mr Cameron and Mr Osborne spun into overdrive, cautioning would-be 'leavers' against taking *a leap into the unknown*, while simultaneously claiming that they knew precisely of what the unknown consisted. A leaflet, written in obscure political jargon, and costing in all over £9 million, was sent by the government to every household in Britain (and thence, one feared, to every recycling bin). Each day's news led off with a new threat. If we voted for what was starting to be called 'Brexit', our action would apparently lose *the pensioners* £138 a year and cost *hard-working families* a total of £4,300. These and other baleful statistics were said to have been supplied by *independent forecasters*, but most appeared to be delivered with the blessing of Treasury Mandarins who had, in common with the rest of the Civil Service, been forbidden to draw up contingency plans against a possible Brexit victory.

Yet the most remarkable thing about Mr Cameron's tactics was how closely, slavishly even, they followed those of Harold Wilson in Labour's 1975 Referendum. Wilson had 'renegotiated' the terms of the 1973 entry into the EEC (by means of a backstairs stitch-up with the West German Chancellor), after which he sought *the verdict of the people* on whether they wished to enter a *reformed* Europe. His parliamentary tactics, as described here by Gordon Brown, also have a familiar ring:

Wilson suspended the convention of collective responsibility for the period running up to the referendum allowing Cabinet members to publicly campaign against each other without being compelled to leave the Government...

Wilson's compromise was messy but mass ministerial resignations were avoided – only the left-winger Eric Heffer resigned after speaking against EEC membership in the House of Commons – and, as Wilson later remarked, the offer of a referendum provided a lifeboat onto which the whole Labour movement could clamber.[2]

The Wilson government also sent out a pamphlet to each household, *Britain's New Deal in Europe*, which set out the aims of the (then) Common Market in terms that were certainly utopian but – unlike the 2016 publication – not exclusively couched in economic language:

♦ To bring together the peoples of Europe.
♦ To raise living standards and improve working conditions.
♦ To promote growth and improve world trade.
♦ To help the poorer regions of Europe and the rest of the world.
♦ To help maintain peace and freedom.

In spite of these fine words, Wilson's own preferred reasons for 'going in' were at base economic. Arguments for the 'out' camp were led by Michael Foot, whose case against membership of the EEC was not based on economic arguments. Instead he argued that staying in would involve a loss of *parliamentary sovereignty*. Imposition of the EEC systems, Foot argued, would be as if 'we had set fire to [the House of Commons] as Hitler had done to the Reichstag'. Cabinet minutes recorded him as warning:

> Continued membership will lead to the dismembering of the United Kingdom, and of the authority of Parliament, which has already lost much of its power in EEC affairs. If we remained in the Community, the seat of power would lie in permanent coalition in Brussels.

And in words that may still resonate with Brexiteers, Foot told the 1975 Labour Party Conference:

> I say to our great country, "Don't be afraid of those who tell us we cannot run our own affairs, that we have not the ingenuity to mobilise our resources and overcome our economic problems."

Foot was however taken ill during the referendum campaign and unable to take any part in it. Speculation about whether the outcome might have been affected if there had been effective opposition is therefore pointless. As it was the Government won comfortably, on a turnout of 68%. The result may suggest that Wilson was a wilier politician than Cameron (with all that implies) but he operated in an easier political environment.

The words of politicians were not then recorded and scrutinised in such detail, the BBC (and the newish ITV) were still quite respectful of the Westminster Establishment – and (crucially) the internet had not been invented.

Forward to 2016. Mr Cameron and his *aide de camp*, Mr George Osborne, went *gung ho* into battle, leading the charge for the 'remain' camp, their ammunition a quiver full of sound bites. There were press photographs of them both, in yellow hard hats, affecting a deep interest in those parts of British industry that a 'leave' vote would, they said, imperil. Almost every day, and in strict rotation, they or their supporters (President Obama, Bob Geldorf, President Hollande, the Chiefs of Staff, Benedict Cumberbatch and a swathe of Subsidised Arts Luvvies) led off news broadcasts with their carefully-crafted – and remarkably similar[3] – injunctions. Mr Osborne concentrated on those 'independent' forecasts of the hellfire that would rain down on us if we were so foolish as to go against his wishes. Mr Cameron became the Uber-Britisher, using one of his favourite verbal tics, the claim that whatever he was promoting at the time was the *right thing to do*. This sometimes emerged in the form of an ancient rhetorical device, known to stump orators and fairground hucksters down the ages as 'the rule of three'. Thus voting to remain became, in Mr Cameron's characteristic bombast, '*right for hard-working families, right for industry and right for Britain*'.

The older political parties sat, with differing degrees of enthusiasm, within the 'remain' camp. The less well organised 'leave' side was also led by politicians, but from widely scattered points across the political spectrum – Mr Gove from the Cabinet, Mr Johnson from the edge of it and Mr Farage, as an MEP and leader of UKIP (the one substantial party committed to leaving). The Referendum thus acquired a second layer of significance. A vote to 'remain' became a vote of confidence not just in Mr Cameron but in the whole Westminster Political Establishment.

Clearly, Mr Cameron expected to win. Most of the press

seemed to expect it as well. The public opinion polls, faced with the awkward (and potentially embarrassing) task of using their delicately weighted samples to forecast the result of what was by its nature a genuine expression of *public opinion* were, at least until the closing stages, also inclined to agree. So it was something of a shock (in headline English, a *bombshell*) when it became clear on the morning of June 24th that – in a high voter turnout of 72% – the UK had voted 52% – 48% to leave the EU.

The resulting brouhaha was no more illuminating than the Referendum campaign had been. Some Establishment figures immediately called for another referendum, claiming that the 'Brexit' side (as 'leavers' were now called) had been misled by the lies told them by their leaders. This was countered by pointing to the lies peddled by the 'Bremain' camp – which included the allegation that voting to leave would *trigger* a Third World War. The Leader of the Liberal Democrat Party slyly suggested that the government should accept the verdict for now, get the best terms they could and *then* put the results to a second referendum – perhaps hoping the conditions for leaving would be rejected, and then the UK could then simply rejoin the EU on its old terms and the whole unfortunate business could safely be forgotten.

Meanwhile things moved rapidly on the domestic front. Mr Cameron, having insisted that whichever way the vote went, he would lead the UK negotiations, promptly resigned the Premiership, and walked back into Number10, humming a gay little tune. His long-serving Home Secretary, Theresa May, was then asked to form a new government. Whereupon Mr Cameron, having assured us that he would definitely stay and contest the next election, also resigned his Parliamentary

Seat. In turn the new Prime Minister, when asked what she was going to do about the result of the Referendum, made her own special contribution to the spirit of the age with her unforgettably frabjous[4] assurance that *'Brexit Means Brexit'*.

Sleight of Hand

Apart from the resignation of the Prime Minister and the relegation of the Chancellor to the back benches, there were a number of other significant shifts in the power struggles within the Establishment. Easiest to comprehend was Mr Farage's (short-lived) resignation from the leadership of UKIP, as he had achieved what had been for many years his major political objective. Less easy to understand was the sudden elevation of Boris Johnson to the post of Foreign Secretary in Mrs May's government. Although the New Minister for Foreign Affairs, Alan Duncan, suggested that a deal had been arrived at which took account of Mr Johnson's devious ambitions:

> I've always thought Boris's wish was to lose by one so that he could be the heir-apparent [to Mr Cameron] without having to have all the… you know, shit of clearing up all the mess. That's always been my view of Boris

BBC Documentary (22 September 2016

Other commentators chose to see Mrs May's placing of the Three Brexiteers (Mr Johnson, Mr Davis and Dr Fox) in key negotiating positions as a cunning political move – though whether it was because she thought they would

approach their task with the zest of the politically committed, or because she suspected that the 'shit of clearing up all the mess' would leave them all bemerded and broken, was not immediately clear.

The broadsheet newspapers – their Business Sections in particular – further blurred the meaning of the word. They began referring to 'Brexit' as if it referred to the *result of the Referendum*, and thus had *already happened*. In their columns we were described as already living in *Post-Brexit Britain*. But in spite of this aberration, the business of preparing a negotiating position for leaving the EU was getting under way. Mrs May made two things clear. First, as 'Article 50' was not going to be *triggered* for some months, negotiations were going to take a considerable time (she was right about that) and second, the UK's negotiating positions were going to be decided away from the gaze of public or parliament (about which she was wrong).

In their meetings, secret or otherwise, the Prime Minister and her fellow plotters would still have to satisfy two seemingly incompatible strands of public opinion. The first was the desire to *regain control of the UK borders*. Second was a wish, extending across parts of both the Brexit and Bremain camps, for the UK to *retain membership of the European Single Market*. How could this circle be squared? The EU Commissioners were adamant that the 'Four Freedoms', of goods, services, people and travel, remained *the cornerstones of the European Union project*.

We have over decades become used to the evasions and half-truths of politicians when they are faced with difficult questions. Their first response is usually to deflect the questioners' attention. Thus particular questions about, for example, management of the local NHS will be batted back with the assurance that *'This Government has given the NHS, year on year, an increase in funding'*. Questions about rotten train services will be deflected by directing the questioner's gaze to the distant horizon; *'We are committed to a fully-operational transport system by 2030.'* The immense social and educational problems that would be raised by a return to providing selective Grammar Schools for some 11-year-olds will be smeared over by the assurance that the proposers believe in raising standards, unlike their opponents who wish to *take us back to the 1970s/1950s/the Stone Age*. The new PM's PR people developed a bland all-purpose rejoinder to any inquiry relating to any political problem; *This government is working hard on a plan which works for everyone*. (Of course they were.)

The second stage in political evasion involves giving a blurred impression of progress being made behind the scenes. We shall be assured (to use a phrase tagged on to almost anything a politician now says) that things are *going forward*

– probably *robustly*. We will be told (with the implication that the question involves complexities we ordinary mortals cannot be expected to grasp) that the politicians are beavering away at their desks, *focusing hard* on the matter, *confronting the problem*, *addressing the issue* and *working unceasingly on its resolution*. These unsung heroes don't just *care* but *care passionately* (sometimes *very passionately*) about the matter but, in case we suspect that they might have succumbed to the temptation to move on, they will offer the stopgap assurances that they must follow *due process*, that lessons have been *learned*, and that *new procedures are being put in place*.

Thirdly, politicians will rename (and in the process redefine) the matters they are supposedly pondering, first as *concerns*, then as *problems*, then *issues* and finally, bringing out of their armory the ultimate weapon, a *challenge* – perhaps even the most momentous challenge of our time. It will immediately replace the challenges of yesteryear – *Rolling Back the Power of the State*; *Education, Education, Education*; *Combating Terrorism*; *Eliminating the Deficit We Inherited from Labour* – which were once all the rage. However as such momentous challenges were usually too big to admit of immediate action – after many years of confronting the *challenges* terrorism was still rampant and the deficit had if anything got larger – they tend to be either postponed more or less indefinitely, or referred to an *Official Inquiry*, which amounts to the same thing.

Unfortunately when she took office Mrs May had to hand none of these well-worn devices for *kicking* the question *into the long grass*. The *people* had already expressed their will. A timetable was already set out in *Article 50* of the EU Constitution. No *Inquiries* could be set up to distract us.

She was left only with the challenge of converting *the will of the people* into action. As an experienced politician she did what she could to shield the political machinations from view. She announced that she was not going to '*give a running commentary on*' (*i.e.* keep Parliament or the people informed of) her Cabinet's ruminations – though strangely, when her Minister in charge of the process, David Davis, gave voice to the commonly-held view that it was highly improbable the UK would be able fully to control its borders *and* retain full membership of the Single Market (21 September 2016), we were told that he was *expressing a personal view*. Which was doubly odd, because if he was *not* following the official government line, then he was acting contrary to the convention of *Collective Cabinet Responsibility*.

If, on the other hand, he *was* following the official line and inadvertently giving away Cabinet secrets, then the Government's mind was engaging at a worryingly primitive level.

The Deputy Prime Minister of the Coalition Government 2010-15, Nick Clegg, took the latter view (19.9.2016):

> You cannot have untrammeled access to a single market, which remember is a single market of rules, without abiding in one shape or other by those rules. That is what will lead to gridlock over the next few years. That is why they find themselves up this Brexit creek, never mind that they don't have a paddle, they don't have a canoe, they don't have a map, they have absolutely no clue whatsoever.

This view was expressed more bluntly by the veteran Tory MP, Ken Clarke, who simply said that the government had no policies for Brexit. Militant Tory Brexiteers meanwhile formed a group, *'Leave means Leave'* , anxious to promote what they called *'a hard exit'* from the EU (although that clarified nothing, as 'leave' can mean either *'get out'* or *'don't touch'*). A group campaigning for a soft exit suggested that negotiations could be so extended that 'Brexit' might drift into *Breconsideration* and in time *Bre-entry* might seem the only sensible course.

For the moment however, all we had was this taunting, *'Brexit means Brexit'*. How were we expected to understand this? In form it sounded rather like a schoolteacher's injunction to an errant pupil ('Brexit *means* Brexit, Montague!'). Or was it a jolly advertising jingle like 'Beanz Means Heinz'? If it meant anything, he likeliest interpretation was that it was a mantra, an incantation of the sort that members of a secret society might intone together at their candlelit meetings and whose metaphorical significance would only be revealed to properly-vetted initiates. Which somehow seemed to fit.

Not of course that there is anything wrong with metaphor as such. As the philosopher Iris Murdoch remarked, we live in myth and symbol all the time, and we make use of it every day to make sense of the world around us. Many great poetic and religious truths are conveyed in metaphor. So are some moral and scientific axioms. Even Mr Clegg's metaphor for Mrs May's dilemma (above) makes its point, though in a tired and flabby way. How much more telling was this stinging denunciation on the vacillations of the Baldwin Government of 1935:

So they go on in strange paradox, decided only to be undecided, resolved to be irresolute. adamant for drift, solid for fluidity, all-powerful to be impotent.

Winston Churchill's soaring rhetoric is highly effective partly because it is composed of memorable images and partly because it so unerringly skewers its intended target. So it is with any good political metaphor. It is still difficult to think of Geoffrey Howe without thinking of *'being savaged by a dead sheep'* or of Michael Howard without recalling there was *'something of the night about him.'* Clarity and context are thus two sides of the same coin. One of the earliest sketches at Peter Cook's Establishment night club in the 1960s showed a worried Foreign Office official peering anxiously at a telegram the FO had just received from the Kremlin: *The geese are rising.* At that time the USSR was very fond of expressing itself in metaphor. But what could it mean? Was it announcing an imminent Russian moon shot? Had the Red Army captured a UK spy? Was it a declaration of war? A new Yoga position favoured by Mrs Kruschev?

To take another example from the satire movement, *Private Eye's* term *Ugandan discussions* is, for the magazine's readers, a well-understood euphemism for illicit sexual congress. This has been in use since the time a lady diplomat from Uganda, claiming to be engaged in 'diplomatic discussions' with a male colleague, was discovered enthusiastically copulating with him in an airport toilet. They may have forgotten the term's origins but *Eye* readers still know exactly to what *Ugandan discussions* refers.

By contrast we shall in the course of this book point to metaphors in our current political language which do not achieve anything like that clarity. The following is an example: Rupert Murdoch's longest-serving editor-in-chief has claimed the News Corp boss was upset by the closeness between his ex-wife Wendi Deng and the former Prime Minister, Tony Blair.

In his memoir *Making Headlines*, Chris Mitchell, the former editor of *The Australian*, has claimed his domestic staff reported this closeness to Rupert Murdoch:

> "It was clear that my boss had been devastated by the *closeness* he found between his wife and his former friend," Mr. Mitchell wrote, "His Australian family, alerted by staff, rang the bell on whatever was going on."
>
> Mr Blair has denied the pair had an affair, while Ms. Deng, rumoured to be in a relationship with Russian President Vladimir Putin, declined to comment.

The *i*, 13 August 2016. [*Our italics.*]

The trouble here is that the coy euphemism *closeness* does not actually tell us what is alleged to have happened. Had Mr Blair and Mrs Murdoch been engaging in *Ugandan discussions*? Or (making use of a distinction now commonly made in everyday speech) did they merely 'have a relationship' – as we all have relationships with our friends and relatives – or were they, like Ms. Deng and Mr Putin, *in a relationship* – a *very* different matter. Mr Blair might have been tempted to follow the fashion of the times and fob off inquirers with an enigmatic phrase (*'Closeness means Closeness'*) but instead tried to close down speculation by simply denying that he and Mrs Murdoch had *had an affair*. So that put an end to the matter. We already knew that we could always trust Mr Blair's word.

Misdirection

In the summer of 2016 we seemed to be sinking into a political quagmire. We, no less than the political Establishment, needed a distraction before we fell prey to depression over the state of our language and our politics. Fortunately just such a distraction was to hand. The Chief Executive of the British Olympic Association, Bill Sweeney, had taken pity on us:

> 'It has been a tough summer, hasn't it? There have been a lot of things happening on the political front, like Brexit. And I think to a certain extent that Brexit did divide the nation. It was pretty much a 50/50 vote really. I think that caused a sense of uncertainty and a little bit of upheaval in the country. And I just think that for sport to do its small piece to reunite the country, and to give you something to cheer about in a British summer, was really good.'

Press Release, 25 August 2016.

The implication was that we had let ourselves down, like squabbling children who'd got a bit over-excited and not behaved as the grown-ups had asked. But we were now being offered the chance of redemption. We could watch the GB athletes on the telly. Then we'd be one big happy family once more!

Although to anyone with a long memory it was somewhat embarrassing that the GB (and Northern Ireland?) team were to gain their successes by means the British press had previously found abhorrent and 'contrary to the Olympic

Spirit'. For nearly half a century, following the 1948 London Olympics, we had railed against the USSR for preparing their athletes for what was supposedly an amateur competition in State Training Camps. Now we were doing the same. Before that we had scorned Adolf Hitler for using German successes in the 1936 Olympic Games to boost the image of the new German Reich. Now we were about to do the same. Though each GB medal had cost us around £4 million, we exulted in the fact that, in the words of the The Daily Telegraph (19.8.2016), Team GB had 'put the Great back in to Great Britain' – a phrase uncomfortably reminiscent of the language which greeted the exploding of the UK's own atomic bomb, 'Today Britain is GREAT BRITAIN again' (Daily Mirror, 4.10.1952). Whenever the press starts to call the UK 'Great Britain' one metaphorically looks around for the nearest parade ground.

By mid-August, less than two months after the Referendum result had been announced, the news was not good. The global refugee crisis was worsening; the numbers of refugees trapped on scorching Greek islands had risen in a month by 150%. Unprecedented floods in Louisiana had caused President Obama to declare a State of Emergency. The *War Against Terror* continued to backfire with *Terrorists* murdering some fifty guests, and injuring two hundred more, when they bombed a Kurdish wedding celebration in Turkey. In the Syrian war pro-Government forces had, in defiance of the UN, dropped napalm bombs on a civilian target, burning a number of their fellow citizens to death.

Yet, in spite of these portentous events, the BBC and the national press had no doubt about what the important 'news' was. Coverage of Britain's participation in the Rio Olympics swamped all other intelligence – to the extent that on the 15th August the first five news pages of *The Daily Telegraph* contained no other stories at all. The BBC meanwhile was devoting the entirety of its short hourly newscasts and a large proportion of its longer news bulletins to the Games – above all to the successes or near-successes of the GB participants. On the 14th August Edward Thomas wrote to the Chairman of the BBC pleading for a 'sense of proportion':

> I can accept [just] the blanket coverage of the Olympics across BBC's 1, 2 and 4. Less tolerable is the predominating effect on the BBC News Channel.
>
> But what is impossible to take is the commandeering of the ordinary news bulletins. Not only has the 10 o'clock news been reduced to 20 minutes but 15 of them are taken up with events in Rio. The rest of the world's news gets the most cursory attention, or even none at all. The evening the Bishop of Derry, Edward Daley, died, there was not a mention of him.

It was unfortunately true that the media coverage of the 2016 Olympics equalled or even surpassed, the empty hysteria of the Referendum. The successful competitors breathlessly assured us that they had *worked really, really hard*, that they were *in the zone, over the moon*, and *living the dream*, that it was all *out of this world, incredible, unbelievable, amazing, fantastic*. No-one resented the athletes' triumphalism, but their exhausted repetitiveness made one suspect that they had no individual emotions at all and were just reaching for off-the-peg cliches, of the sort we abhorred when shouted by drugged-up clubbers on a Friday night:

I'm on a cloud. Its incredible, amazing, really, really fantastic. Everybody's messaging me and I'm like… Wee – ee – eh!

Which were the words athlete Dame Sarah Storey used in a BBC interview (7 September 2016) to describe her delight at winning an Olympic event. A few days later Mrs May's new Culture Secretary, Karen Bradley, said that although Manchester United, The Beatles, Coldplay, Adele, *Downton Abbey*, *Strictly Come Dancing* and *Top Gear* were already totems of GB culture (*sic*), the Rio Olympics had been an *'incredible experience'*, making Great Britain *the **envy** of the world*. Amongst the GB athletes there were no villains, only *heroes* and *superheroes*, about whom no story, however banal, was deemed unworthy of a few column inches:

DUJARDIN SAYS 'YES' AGAIN TO MARRIAGE PROPOSAL AS SHE WINS GOLD MEDAL

As Charlotte Dujardin rode to victory in Rio, taking gold in the individual dressage, there was one burning question on the scoreboard – a marriage proposal from her partner... as the scoreboard revealed her winning total, it also brandished a handmade banner from her partner, Dean Golding, asking "Can we get married now?"

The 31-year-old remained unperturbed, pointing out that they were already engaged, after an initial proposal in 2008.

She said, "He already knows it's yes. He's already asked me, he's just looking for me to say 'yes' more."

The *i*, (16 August 2016)

Sophie Roebuck of Bury St Edmunds urged in the same newspaper that the honours should be more widely shared. 'Nowhere,' she complained, 'in the celebrations around gymnast Max Whitlock has his hairdresser been mentioned... whether he was standing or upside down, his hair stayed immaculate.'

Even the suspicion that Sophie Roebuck (for David Cameron had recently nominated his wife's hairdresser for an honour) just might have been writing tongue-in-cheek, could not disguise the gratitude felt by the political establishment for the massive distraction provided by the televised athletics. And when it was all over we read (*The Guardian*, 17th September 2016) that the Rio Olympics had, like the London Olympics of 2012, been *an inspiration to millions*. Although it was perhaps useful to remember that for most of those newly-inspired millions it had in fact been an extended television show – something people watched on their iPads, or from the depths of their own sofas – possibly refreshing themselves with their accustomed diet of crisps, burgers, pizzas and a few cans of neck oil. For, even as the newspapers exulted in GB's athletic glory you could read on the inside pages that the incidence of clinical obesity in the nation's youth had, since the fabled inspiration of the 2012 Olympics, risen by some 8%. And over the same period use of hard drugs in the UK had risen by 66%. So, when a young person said admiringly of another that he/she is *fit* or *well fit*, it is important that future historians remember that *fit* was a slang term of the period and do not fall into the trap of thinking that in 2016 they meant that the person referred to was *ready to compete in an Olympic event*. Or ready to vote in a Referendum, come to that.

[1] Robin Cook, *The Point of Departure*, Pocket Books 2004, p.172

[2] Gordon Brown, *Britain: Leading not Leaving*, Deerpark Press 2016, p.87.

[3] The similarity of these bombastic slogans is generally attributed to the influence that the Tory Party's advertising guru, Lynton Crosby, was said to wield.

[4] For the definitive meaning of frabjous see *Jabberwocky* by Lewis Carroll.

2

THE AFTERSHOCK

It's not the world that's got so much worse, but news coverage that's got so much better.
G. K. Chesterton

It is startling to find *freedom of the press* subsumed under *freedom of doing business. The first freedom of the press consists in it not being a business.*
Karl Marx, reviewing *Les Mysteres de Paris*, 1879

The simulation game Football Manager, where players take control of the day-to-day running of a club, is to add new layers of difficulty by asking players to deal with Brexit. The vote to leave the EU is too significant to omit.
Sports Interactive (Developers)

We now consider how far the fragmented rhetoric of the Referendum hustings could be said to be symptomatic of a wider malaise – the implosion of our political language, no less. Have we lost the ability to engage in serious political discussion? Is the question posed in the 2016 Referendum, given the present state of things, now *impossible* to answer conscientiously?

The basic conditions for holding any national referendum in the UK would seem to be a) that the accredited voters understand the question, b) that they all have a means of casting their votes, c) that the poll is properly supervised, and d) the result honestly recorded. In the 2016 Referendum the conditions b), c) and d) were no doubt properly met. There were, it is true, a few initial worries over who should be included in the roll call of accredited voters. In the 2014 Scottish Referendum, teenagers had been eligible to vote if they had passed their sixteenth birthday before polling day (an innovation which the winning side, who benefited from the young people's support, considered had been thoroughly justified). However, after toying briefly with the idea of adopting that same practice in the UK-wide 2016 Referendum, the government came out firmly against it.

So we turn to a much greater difficulty, and ask whether the voters could have been said to 'understand the question'. Now if that simply means, could everybody grasp the meaning of the words? – then the answer is 'probably, yes'. Nor could any syntactical difficulty have presented itself, in what was a simple binary choice, albeit one which might involve a bit of mulling over. For it seemed on the surface to be no more intricate than being asked, say, 'Do you want to remain in, or to leave your present pension scheme?' And if it *had* been something of that order, voters might have expected to have received one of those carefully crafted information sheets that Fund Managers are obliged by law to produce, setting out the consequences of remaining in, or leaving, their scheme. But it soon became clear that the considerations involved could not be summarised on a sheet of A4. Voters learned that this

deceptively simple question rested on an intricate patchwork of economic, political, social, legal, educational, military, cultural and industrial considerations which, even when examined in depth, yielded no simple answer. Yet the Referendum question was stark; '*In*' or '*Out*'?

When the question had first been announced, there had been little newspaper comment. Few, if any, took exception to its wording. In fact – to be frank – there wasn't much interest at all. It seemed to many people that it was just another political wheeze coming from a Prime Minister who had a liking for cunning stunts. And even when it became clear that the question was too simply phrased, there was no demand that it be reworded, or that the Referendum be cancelled. A torpor had descended upon the land, and UK voters, at first, viewed the proposed Referendum in much the same light as they had viewed many of Mr Cameron's previous initiatives, as something set up to distract them from the effects of the government's austerity programme. To counter this apathy right wing politicians began to raise the stakes, suggesting that it was *the most important question we would be faced with in our lifetimes.* Our *children* and our *children's children* would never forgive us if we didn't participate in its resolution. We should, for the sake of our families, our futures (and our Financial Services), get out there and play our allotted parts.

Then all sorts of verbal flak – slogans, statistics, catchphrases, threats and promises – began to rain down upon us. Which may be the moment to remind ourselves just how relentless – even in normal times – this blitzkrieg of information has become. Visual, musical and verbal messages now bombard us throughout our waking moments. We have rolling 'news' 24 hours a day, incessantly relayed to us by radio, television, laptop, smartphone and iPad. This *ongoing* 'news service', for the most part an amalgam of speculation, rumour and celebrity gossip, has itself become a species of soap opera, with its own heroes and villains, interwoven plot lines and comedy relief. Together with online games and *messaging* friends and followers it forms for many people a simulacrum of real life which we shall henceforth in these pages call *Electronic Reality.*[1]

In that bloodless realm a large number of our fellow citizens now live their lives. Their virtual 'friends' are distant acquaintances, and their 'followers' an assorted mixture of people with a corresponding assortment of motives. Yet young people in particular will now often talk of these electronic images with more emotion than they speak of their real-life friends and followers. And, although they have never met them, or seen them at work, it is common nowadays to hear someone say they *love* or *hate* a contemporary politician or 'personality'.Or, even if they have never been near to White Hart Lane and live in Gibraltar, that they *support* Tottenham Hotspur.[2] It is important to keep in mind that a great many people now gather information, form allegiances and shape their opinions almost entirely from this virtual world, constructing an existence more real to them than the world of flesh and blood. And during the Referendum debate, for such people, a sort of 'news' emerged from their regular immersion in this *Electronic Reality* – although it was not 'news' as we had once known it.

'News'

'Now, what news on the Rialto?' Salanio's question to Salarino in Shakespeare's *The Merchant of Venice* (1595) uses the term 'news' in its ordinary Elizabethan sense, to mean 'the latest information'. Such 'news' in Shakespeare's plays is always spoken. For example, in *Macbeth* (1606), the hero is taunted throughout, even at his final descent into hell, by the 'news' that messengers bring to him. That 'news' is always the truth, and is to be sharply distinguished from gossip and rumour. The murderous Macbeth for example gives short shrift to the gossip relayed to him by one of King Duncan's entourage (Act 2 Scene 3):

LENNOX: The night hath been unruly;. Where we lay,
Our chimneys were blown down; and, as they say,
Lamentings heard i'the air; strange screams of death,

And prophesying with accents terrible
Of dire combustion and confus'd events
New hatch'd to the woeful time. The obscure bird
Clamoured the livelong night: some say the earth
Was feverous and did shake.

MACBETH: 'Twas a rough night.

It is not until Ben Jonson's *The Staple of News* (1631) that we have our first mention of printed 'news'. The seventeenth-century newsbooks the play satirises were indeed simple confections, containing a mixture of information, rumour and comment. With tiny circulations, they were considered to be at best a novelty supplement to the more reliable spoken news that could be heard in the inns and courts of London. Yet already, as one of Jonson's characters remarks:

See divers men's opinions: unto some
The very printing of 'em makes them news:
They have not the heart to believe any thing,
But what they see in print.

So, in the printed news of the seventeenth century, rumour and gossip are already mixed up with plain reportage. By the end of the eighteenth century, the venality of the press was already the subject of ridicule.[3] A century later, free of the newspaper taxes, employing roller presses to print in tens of thousands and with nationwide distribution made possible by the new steam trains, the national daily newspapers assumed a new political importance. First, by reporting the opinions of politicians, and secondly by offering their own editorial commentary on events – as this memoir of C. P. Scott, the long-serving Editor of *The Manchester Guardian,* recalls:

> No interruption, no visitor, no office conference was allowed to delay the sacred task of fixing for the night the subject of "the Long".This was the Long Leader, prime instrument of policy, the voice, persuasive or protestant, for whose utterance, more than any other single purpose, he believed the newspaper to exist.[4]

Politicians now began to court the press, in the expectation that they could thereby discover, and influence, the existing state of public opinion. They started to employ what were in effect *Public Relations* men. 1895 saw the setting-up of what became the first full-time Government *Information Unit*, in the Board of Education. The post of Chief Officer was advertised in these terms:

> There is a large number of matters affecting education as to which the Department lives merely from hand to mouth, failing to record the knowledge it obtains for future use, and unable to obtain information as to what is being done elsewhere, whether at home or abroad, in an efficient manner. There is now such a waste of power through this deficiency that the appointment of an officer... whose duty it shall be to collect and supply information and to make occasional reports in special matters... has become essential.

Thereafter political PRs grew in importance. 'News' was now being created by means of a business compact, in which politicians and their agents conspired with editors to determine what was to be disclosed to the general public. It was usually a joint endeavour, but sometimes an editor towered above the politicians – most notably the formidable Lord Northcliffe. In the words of his biographer:

> He was immensely important, however much solemn people might try to blink or evade the fact. He and his imitators influenced the common mind more than all the Education Ministers put together... In a sense he was the only completely convinced democrat I ever knew. He really did believe that things ought to be decided by mass opinion about them... [5]

In the twentieth century newspapers lost their monopoly of 'news', first to radio, then television, then to the new *social media*. As a result of the competition between them 'news' also changed its nature. It became not just a record of past events, but some politician's *opinion* of a coming one. This habit has grown to the extent that 'news' is not just a forecast of what politicians will say, but of what they will disagree about. This means even in the more respectable news channels, the 'news' is often composed of pure speculation. It is quite reasonable that *pledges* (such the one David Cameron gave, prior to the 2010 election, that there would be no third runway built at Heathrow) should be considered newsworthy, but quite unreasonable for the 'news' on BBC Radio 4 to lead (21.10.16) on Mrs May's bland assertion that the following year's negotiations to leave the EU would have 'difficult moments'.And there was no excuse for the ensuing media speculation about whether this had put her *on a collision course* with Mrs Merkel, who had opined that the

2017/18 negotiations would be 'tough'. That is speculation raised to the level of fantasy.

In the last twenty years or so, our means of receiving all kinds of information, including 'news', has changed dramatically. In Mark Dooley's words

> Electronic engagement has made it possible to defy natural boundaries in a way inconceivable to our forebears... In such a 'world' individuals are not defined by language, religion or place. Identities are established on Facebook and in 'chat rooms', virtual congregations where countless communicants are bound by a common host... There is no past nor future in cyberspace, only a perpetual 'now' in which all desires must be instantly gratified. It is a no man's land devoid of the public-private distinction... where no one can hide.[6]

In the contemporary UK almost everybody now has the means – by smartphone or smartpad, iPhone or iPad – to record and transmit anything that happens around them as 'news'. They can, using the same technologies, also *create* or *edit* 'news' –a street accident, a flash dance in Red Square, or an intimate movie of themselves having sex (as one of the medal-winning *Olympic heroes* did this summer). Moreover, in the absence of any agreed standards, anyone can now manipulate and mangle the English language at will. So in this new world of *Electronic Reality*, it is tempting to invent a new political slogan; '*We proles are the Big Brothers now*'.

Some political movements seemed able to make use of the new social media, blending their messages in with what was *trending* to further their own ends. *Populist* movements, in particular, now target Facebook's 1.79 billion users to pillory their political enemies. Such a one was President Trump whose tweets were more respectfully reported during (and after) his Presidential campaign than anything he said at his rallies. Trump and his campaign managers, in concert with social media, were thus able to gather up, and inflame the gripes of contemporary America about subjects as diverse as job losses, the Clinton Dynasty, drug dealers, Mexican immigrants, steel imports from China and servicemen serving overseas. Like most contemporary *populists*, Trump offered no high *aspirations*, but instead offered his followers a common enemy, a cause of all their ills – *the liberal Washington Establishment.*

Sometimes it works in the opposite direction, and the common enemy – *youth, immigration, global warming, the liberal metropolitan elite* – is already implanted in the voters' minds, and stands ready to be used as a scapegoat for any unwelcome event. We could witness this process in our national press. A newspaper could slowly implant in its readers the belief that there existed in the UK a common enemy – a large class of persons that lived in permanent luxury on state handouts, and used their state-funded leisure time idly to procreate and do hard drugs. Then it only required one or two (real or invented) stories each week – the woman with thirteen children who lives in luxury on child benefits, the immigrant who drives a Roller and peddles smack – to keep the 'threat' alive in readers' minds.

But, as President Trump has shown, nowadays scapegoats are created much more quickly and by other and more insidious means.

Electronic Reality

A young acquaintance remarked the other day that she was in a good mood because a gentleman friend had that morning sent her a bunch of flowers. It gradually became clear that the sender was one of her Facebook 'friends', and that the two of them had never, in fact, actually met. Moreover the 'flowers' were an emoji. So what had happened was that one iPhone image had 'sent' to another iPhone image an iPhone pictograph of a bunch of flowers. The lady was nevertheless quite chuffed about this. (Well, it wouldn't do if we were all the same.) Our only reaction was that it would serve as an illustration of the silent revolution which has transformed so many people's lives.

Older people like ourselves are at various times intrigued by, even slightly resentful of, new methods of electronic communication. We marvel at the speed at which these personal devices – the smartphone, the iPad, the laptop – have become for so many younger people such an essential adjunct to everyday living. And we have become used, in pubs or restaurants where ordinary conversation once flowed, to seeing everybody in the room staring down at their laps and fiddling with their dimly glowing screens. On our pavements we are facing a new hazard from *Deadwalkers,* the term recently coined by the *Washington Post* to describe people who walk the streets while looking down at their mobile phones, oblivious of other pedestrians. Or of traffic. (Or cliff edges?)

In not much more than a decade these electronic devices have rendered the postal services, the camera, the manual typewriter and the telegram virtually obsolete. They have helped to change the nature of broadcasting, newspapers, the public libraries, universities, encyclopedias, schools, the cinema, courtship, games, street protests and much, much else. Almost three quarters of the British population now own one or more of these devices, and on average their users spend more than one whole day *a week* communing with them. Research suggests that, in descending order of importance, they occupy these twenty seven on-line hours by:

Texting, and reading texts
Browsing other people's social media profiles
Checking their own social media channels
Browsing the internet (to see what's trending
Playing games on iPhone
Researching holidays (that may never be taken)
Watching animal videos online

More than a third of users sleep with their devices on their bedside table so that as soon as they wake they can discover who has *messaged* them, and what's newly *trending*. Access to this alternative realm continues to grow apace. The social analysts *CCS Insight* claimed (November 2016) that by 2020 we in the UK will have purchased 21 million *Virtual Reality* platforms and a further 72 million *smartphone* devices. The size and speed of this technological revolution is without precedence.

The language used to describe activity in this new *Electronic Reality* is itself alarming, for it describes the use of such gadgets as if they were activities being undertaken in the real human world. Users are said to have a strong *Facebook presence,* and are said to *go on to* it, or *visit* it. They *trawl* for information on the net and collect *followers* and *friends* by purely electronic means. A further clue to the nature of this 'reality' lies in the everyday conversation of the young, some of whom seem to have dispensed altogether with the conventions of reported speech. No longer do they say, for example, 'My friend said I should dye my hair blonde, so I asked why?', but instead '*She's like, you should dye your hair blonde, and I'm like* (voice rising in crescendo) *Wha-a-at!!!*' The last word will probably be acted full-on, with the mouth hanging incredulously open and the eyes widened in an exaggerated goggle. By these means the speaker dramatises and objectifies herself. It is almost as if she is reporting the actions of someone else. As in a sense, she is.

Even the most reluctant of us may from time to time be forced to employ the tools of *Electronic Reality,* but for many it is their permanent home. And for such people, the

view they form of the real human world is fashioned by an accretion of words and images largely culled from the *social media*. So the politicians involved in the Referendum hustings, in spite of their protestations of honesty and truthfulness, and in spite of the efforts of their PR staffs, sometimes found that their 'images' (a venerable but still useful word) worked against them.

To take the obvious example, few people have any first-hand knowledge of Mr Cameron, but a large number of people hold strong opinions about him. The 'David Cameron' they know is formed in part from seeing him trumpeting forth his pledges and assertions on the television news, in part from cartoons and comic strips (*The simpleton with a condom on his head,* 'Dave Snooty and His Pals') from the relentless trending of his gaffes (a red-faced Dave forgetting whether it was Aston Villa or Queens Park Rangers or some other football club that he 'supported') and from the more fanciful on-line parodies that followed upon the (alleged) *closeness* between Mr Cameron and a dead pig's head, or the Sunday lunchtime he inadvertently left one of his children in a Cotswolds pub. But whatever may have helped to create this image of our (then) Prime Minister, during the Referendum campaign his minders would not allow him to debate directly on television with Boris Johnson, who was thought (rightly or wrongly) to have a more cuddly appeal.

Yet if their image of the Prime Minister was fragmented, how much more confused were voters' images of 'The European Union', 'The City', 'The National Debt', 'British Industry' or any of the other concepts bandied about during the Referendum hustings? Shot through as they were with charges and counter-charges of racism, economic illiteracy, lack of patriotic feeling and indifference to our grandchildren's futures. And, sad to relate, post-Referendum, the terms of the debate became no clearer. On the contrary. On 26th October, Mrs May, in reply to a question from Jeremy Corbyn, uttered the unforgettable phrase, *"Brexit means Brexit" means leaving the EU"* – thus achieving that precious rarity in English syntax – **a *triple tautology!***

[1] There are many other names for this oppressive modern phenomenon. The Irish philosopher Mark Dooley calls it *Cyberia.*

[2] It is strange to see how often our status is defined by our taste in pop music, and by what football team we support. If you say you do not have a particular yen for any pop group, you are thought to be from another planet. One of us was recently asked at a civic reception, as an ice-breaker, which football team they supported? It seemed so fey and other-worldly to answer (truthfully) 'none'.

[3] See Sheridan's *The Critic,* 1779.

[4] L. Hammond,*C. P. Scott,* Bell 1927, p.132

[5] J. A. Spender, *Life, Journalism and Politics,* Cassell 1921, p.227

[6] Mark Dooley, *Conserving the Sacred in a Virtual Kingdom* in *What's Wrong With Us?* Imprint Academic, 2016. p.208

3

WHAT ARE THEY SAYING?

The wrinkly bastards stitched us young 'uns up good and proper. From their stairlifts and their Zimmer frames, their electric beds and their walk-in baths, they reached out with their wizened old writing hands to make their wobbly crosses and screwed their children and their children's children for a thousand generations.

Giles Coren, quoted in *The Oldie*, on learning that elderly people voted for Brexit.

If the apocalyptic predictions of George Osborne and his Project Fear cohorts had come to pass, Britain would now be spiralling into recession. How strange than, that we are seeing almost exactly the opposite. So the mystifying question is how could so many economic 'experts' get it so egregiously wrong, and why were they so adamant that Brexit would lead to catastrophe?

The Guardian Editorial **28 October 2016**

It's been a rough year. Now, more than ever, we need to curl up on the sofa and watch other people making cakes.

Michael Moran, *CNN*, after 15 million people had watched the final of *The Great British Bake Off*

The months between the announcement of the Referendum result and the *triggering* of *Article 50* did not, unfortunately, herald a return to balanced commentary and cool disinterested analysis. If anything, political language became even more confused. There were more transitive verbs awkwardly fashioned from intransitive ones – 'Dan Smith *grew* his ball-bearing business last year' – and a lot more verbs clumsily spawned from nouns or adjectives. So people continued to *message* each other, and a spokesperson complained, post Brexit, 'We Muslims have been *otherised*' (14 November, 2016). Civil servants were still *tasked* with preparing negotiating positions, and still *trialled* their ill-thought-out responses, *signposted* the way forward and *highlighted* the outcome. In their turn politicians, conscious that they were interpreting or subverting *the will of the people*, or acting in ways contrary to the position they had taken during the Referendum debate, insisted with renewed vigour that they had always been *clear,* often *very clear,* and sometimes *very, very clear* about movements or entities about which the denizens of Westminster *spoke passionately,* such as *hard-working families, ambitious apprentices, the squeezed middle, the just-about-managing,* though they seemed to have no corporeal existence out in the real world.

Some old journalistic habits remained in evidence – notably that mystic ability instantly to divine collective emotions surging through the populace; *Everywhere in Europe, people are angry.* This awesome journalistic power was evident in such headlines as '*Fresh Anger over Boris's Boobs*', or '*Frustration over May's Secret Assignation with Motor Head*'. Sometimes journalists even sensed emotions were bubbling up towards a climax which, if it had ever

come to pass, would have been horrible to contemplate – *'Fury Erupts over Brexit Fudge'*. Though, oddly enough, we never had reports of these mob feelings receding. Perhaps old journalistic hands felt that *'Anger Waning in Whitehall'* would, like *'The Government is Ordering No New Clampdowns this Morning'*, sell few newspapers.

It was not just in the headlines that such hyperbole could be read. It was also to be found in the political reporting, in which political transgressions were never just investigated but *probed,* governments did not simply forbid things but *outlawed* them, simultaneously *triggering* a major *clampdown*, during which concerns were routinely *voiced,* beliefs were *beggared* and surprises invariably *sprung.* In this ceaseless recycling of journalistic cliché, the most mundane of the government's actions took on a manic air, as politicians variously *ruled out, underlined, set aside, drew a line under, reached out to, confronted* and *moved into line with* the various strategies *under consideration* for leaving the EU.

Political oratory meanwhile seemed to be a dying art. There was no Churchill, no Bevan, no Foot and no Powell to lift or inflame the spirits. Few of the remaining *Big Beasts* – Ken Clarke and Dennis Skinner excepted – could still command attention. Only a handful of other politicians – Jacob Rees-Mogg, Nigel Farage, Jeremy Corbyn, Boris Johnson – still made ripples by what they did, or didn't, say. But, as the Prime Minister's substitution of abuse for answers at Prime Minister's Questions indicated, Parliament itself now disdained clear argument. Debate in the House of Commons seemed to consist of Members angrily shouting their well-worn clichés, then lowing like cattle at the same phrases when they were trotted out by the other side.

Surely the truth was that in the UK much of the old political language was breathing its last, and many of its key words were dying of overuse, too far gone to be resuscitated by firm redefinition.. We pause now to glance at five common political *buzzwords* which over recent years have had the last drop of meaning wrung out of them:

<u>Policy</u> In the nineteenth century the word meant trickery or deceit. Thus it was that early Victorian governments had a *Foreign Policy* (to deal with duplicitous Johnny Foreigner) but no discrete Education or Health Policy. It later came to mean 'mission' or 'intention'. Not so long ago a policy was still a guide to future action, but nowadays a 'policy' is little more than a marketing tool, indistinguishable from an advertising slogan. '*We have a robust Equal Opportunities policy in place,*'

the Company's Managing Director will proclaim, hoping that we might overlook the fact that its Board and Senior Management are still largely composed of white middle-aged males.

<u>Terrorism</u> Any organised group which aims to achieve its political ends by imposing a Reign of Terror upon the populace can be said to be engaged in terrorism. The term is now wrongly used in the UK as if it can apply only to those of foreign extraction. Yet the UK itself has on occasion allied itself with terrorist techniques to achieve its political ends – during the Boer War for instance, at the dropping of the atomic bomb on Hiroshima or in the 'Shock and Awe' strategy used for the invasion of Iraq. Nor is it a word which can unthinkingly be applied to activities which aim to be no more than mildly disruptive – rockers, goths, football hooligans, installation artists and the like.

<u>Democracy</u> The word, and its practical application, supposedly derives from fifth century B.C. Athens – but we do not in practice mirror their democratic *system,* for in the Athenian state only men with full citizenship took part in political affairs; their wives and daughters having only limited rights, while their thousands of slaves had none at all. After the French Revolution, the word acquired another, broader, meaning; 'Government for the people by the people'. This was in turn trashed by President George Bush, who claimed after 9/11 that part of his mission was to 'spread Democracy' – though he applied the term to any country which held an occasional election and was willing to buy US arms. Taking advantage of his permissive ignorance a number of quasi-

military dictatorships, such as Thailand, Afghanistan, Nigeria and Iraq, began to call themselves Democracies. The Turkish Government recently prosecuted or imprisoned more than 40,000 citizens, and arrested over 100 journalists, saying that by doing so it was *defending Democracy.*

Sovereignty This word no longer refers to a Monarch's power over his or her realm, and in recent decades has come variously to mean 1) The unrestricted power of the state, 2) The autonomy of a Sovereign, or sovereign power, and 3) An independent state. These separate, interlocking, definitions are all invoked by the contemporary use of the term, so that a discussion of, say, Palestine, Crimea or Ireland in terms of their past or future 'sovereignty' will only add to the prevailing confusion. In the UK the word brings to mind causes as varied as *Scottish Nationalism, Republicanism, the Need to Keep Out Refugees, Devolution* and *Nationhood* – so that it clarifies nothing. Indeed 'Sovereignty' is not now considered a useful political term, even in the General Assembly of the UN.

Liberal Quite apart from the fact that it was once the name of a significant political party, the word 'liberal' until quite recently conveyed a sense of breadth, a generous open-mindedness. The authors, for instance, have at various times taught in 'Liberal Studies Departments', in which a broad curriculum was taught in the cause of general enlightenment. In recent years however it has become for some politicians (particularly in the US) a term of abuse, meaning *permissive, slightly camp and over-concerned with the plight of the needy.* In the UK Mrs May has recently invented a new enemy, the

'*Liberal, Metropolitan Elite*' which does not of course exist, but which puts the mockers on ever using the word again.

These are a few examples of terms still used as clinchers in political debate but which, sadly, are now too worn and faded to be meaningfully deployed. There are many others, even including the once-noble term *freedom*, to which we turn in the next section.

Political Correctness

Our political language has in recent decades also come under threat from 'political correctness' – which can be defined as the prohibition of any political or social opinion that is perceived to be contrary to current linguistic mores. Its reach extends from the censoring of nursery tales (*Little Black Sambo*) through play titles (*Ten Little Indians*) and thence to the far more serious crime of UK university students boycotting or *No platforming* speakers with whose views they think they ought to disagree.

The justification for the latter practice usually runs along the lines of *Freedom cannot be absolute, and there must be limits imposed.* Yes indeed, freedom of *action* must always have bounds set upon it, but freedom of *thought*? If we are not allowed to know and consider the views and feelings of Seventh Day Adventists, Fascists, Flat Earthers or Anti-Abortionists, and anyone else who may have an allegiance different from our own, how can we reflect upon them and thus come to know ourselves? And how can we know who are our real enemies? We will only know nations or people as our adversaries because somebody has tied some derogatory label to them. They are to be fought and defeated because they are labelled *communists, terrorists, bigots, colonialists, racists* or whatever. They will know us as their enemies because they in turn are told that we are *blasphemers, capitalists, infidels* or *decadent scum.* In preparing to do battle with them we will pride ourselves that we are *freedom-lovers, democrats, peace-loving, patriotic* and *right-minded.* Which are precisely the kind of terms our adversaries also use about themselves.

When *political correctness* forbids us from using common words (which we all know, but do not use in polite society) for *one born out of wedlock, a native of Pakistan, a habitual user of hard drugs, a person who frequently indulges in masturbation,* or *a woman who is too liberal with her favours* then the forbidden words will soon be replaced by alternative slang terms. Unfortunately as soon as a new slang term becomes widely understood it too becomes *politically incorrect,* so the process continues in ever-decreasing circles. Alternately the new slang may be confined to particular groups (members of the Armed Forces, a teenage tribe or players of a particular sport) who keep the meanings private so that even if by chance they do leak into the public realm, the general public cannot know whether the word refers to *a bastard, a Paki, a druggie, a wanker, a slag* or, mayhap, to a newly discovered species of butterfly. Indeed we are minting new words at an unprecedented rate so that people from different areas of the country, people from different professions and indeed people from different age groups find it increasingly hard to speak to, or understand, each other.

In 2016 among the fifty or so newly-minted words appearing in *Collins Dictionary* were *Brexit* (of course), *Dude Food, Hygge, jomo, sharenting* and *throw shade.* The meaning of some of these may be deduced by etymologists or crossword fanatics, though newly-minted slang words which have not yet come to the notice of the dictionary compilers present a much greater challenge. New words are sometimes particular to one locality. In the South East, where the authors happen to live, we have recently learned of *pasties* and *candles* who are finding things *sick* but are *bricking it* for fear of being *dragged* by *hoolies.* We shall not arrange for a translation, as by the time the book is published, new words will have taken their place. Local slang changes with the moons.

'Political correctness' also changes, though not with the same bewildering rapidity. Within our lifetimes for example it was thought proper to refer to 'coloured', but not to 'black' people. Now 'black' is the polite term to use and 'coloured' is an insult. 'Brother', once a term used of a fellow Union member, has now been appropriated (sometimes shortened to 'Bro') by black men to describe their black male friends. The ways we allude to mentally-ill or physically disadvantaged people have changed even more often. Some of these shifts in terminology may pass us by, but there is still a social penalty if, in our ignorance, we refer wrongly to any group. There is an understandable fear of being behind the fashion, of using a politically incorrect term and inadvertently giving offence. An elderly lady of our acquaintance was recently relaying news of a mutual friend. 'She's now gone blind, poor old duck,' she told us, and then looked anxiously around her before asking, 'Is it all right to say *blind*?'

The fear of being thought to be *politically incorrect* may lie behind the curious practice of 'colour blind casting' in our subsidised theatres. Writing in the theatrical magazine *Encore* (July 2005) Edward Thomas put the case against it clearly:

Casting directors and producers spend an inordinate amount of time deciding who is too short, tall, old, young, and on a whole range of characteristics in selecting actors for parts. Yet one characteristic to which they are oblivious, or – one strongly suspects – are required to be on account of political correctness, is the one that is more obvious than most: the skin color of their actors and actresses.

Nicholas Hytner is currently Artistic Director of the National Theatre and under his stewardship a similar piece of fantasy was played out two years ago with the casting of Adrian Lester in the title role of Henry V. Mr Lester is a first-rate actor, his performance as Bobby in the revival of Stephen Sondheim's 'Company' at the Donmar Warehouse could not be faulted, nor was it inauthentic. Here was a black man with a number of mostly white friends in New York – a situation that was feasible. But Adrian Lester portrayed Henry V, as white a role as one could imagine.[1]

Among the reactions to Mr Thomas's observations was one from the (then) Chief Executive of the Birmingham Hippodrome, Stuart Griffiths, who made it quite clear that mere *authenticity* (presenting the action credibly) took second place to the 'political correctness' of 'colour blind casting'. He wrote:

> Edward Thomas might quote the fact that Adrian Lester was cast in 'Company' but he also stated that he shouldn't play Henry V in the cause of 'authenticity'. Is he really saying that thousands of roles should not be available to actors who are not white? If he is then I am astonished that he still holds such abhorrent views and sickened that he chooses to advocate them in print . . . Racism is evil and we have to work hard together as an industry to eliminate it – supposed lack of authenticity I can live with.[2]

Although whether Mr Griffiths can live with it is surely irrelevant. The real question is whether, in order to appease the social conscience of the manager, members of an audience can be made, in defiance of their senses, to pretend to be 'colour blind'? Surely not. The theatregoer's mind looks to understand and interpret what it directly sees upon a stage, and does not pass it through a prism of political correctness. In a much-praised London production of *King Lear* a few years ago, Derek Jacobi played the eponymous hero and Lear's youngest daughter was played by a black actress. It was surely impossible for members of the audience to stop themselves from wondering why nobody in Lear's entourage commented on the fact that Cordelia was black. Had the King married twice? Been playing away? *Adopted* her? As Lear's Queen does not appear in the play, it might have made better sense to cast black actresses in the roles of all three daughters, but having just one black child was nonsense not least, as Brian Freeland points out, because infidelity is a sub-plot of the play.[3]

The tone of Mr Griffiths' letter is illustrative of another uncomfortable fact – that people who challenge political correctness, or similar political fashions, will nowadays run the risk of being vilely and grotesquely abused. Mr Thomas's calmly argued views are said to be 'abhorrent' and in expressing them he is stigmatized as 'racist' and 'evil'. And Mr Griffiths does not just disagree with him, but professes to be '*sickened*'. Yet does the mild tone of Mr Thomas's commentary really warrant such a hysterical reaction? Is there not some deeper, unacknowledged tension at work here?

On a different level, Gina Miller (November, 2016) successfully challenged the Government in the High Courts over its decision not to allow Parliament the right to debate the UK negotiating positions for the EU talks. In court her counsel had, quite properly, referred to the long-established UK constitutional practice of the 'separation of powers', by which the Executive may not ride roughshod over the judiciary. But Ms Miller, whose actions throughout were within the law, faced an immediate torrent of online abuse, including threats of extreme physical violence, murder and gang rape.

Post-Truthfulness

Political language is quickly disintegrating. Long-established political terms have been so bruised and battered that they now have to be accompanied by a string of disclaimers; *I am old Labour, but in spite of Jeremy's views I want to keep Polaris, though I certainly don't want Blair back,* etc. *I have always been Tory but I'm pro EU and I'd prefer it if Boris were not Foreign Secretary,* etc, etc.

Amid this confusion there is one final, massive obstacle to meaningful political dialogue – in so many ways the most formidable barrier of all. It is the fact that powerfully-composed (albeit untrue or meaningless) slogans, transmitted through the social media, will nowadays *resonate* with the public far more effectively than the truth. Constant repetition propels these manufactured slogans into everyday speech, so that such phrases come to combine the unnerving power of rally slogans with the insidious rhythm of an advertising jingle. (As a consequence contemporary political slogans sometimes sound like the titles of popular wartime songs: 'Ladies and Gentlemen, let's hear it for that old forces' favourite, *We're Stronger Together* followed by *Let's Take Our Country Back!* All together now!')

In 2005 Stephen Colbert coined the word *truthiness* for those slogans which, at the time, 'feel right in the gut', even though they have little basis in fact. The term can be used, slightly disparagingly, of those teachers, or novelists, who aspire to guru status and who, tapping their chests meaningfully, will tell their followers that they *feel* something is right/wrong *here*. It could be used to describe those stage performers who claim to be giving *truthful* performances, when they mean something more like *dramatically plausible.* But above all it is a useful term to describe politicians who speak, emphatically and repeatedly 'from the gut', telling us (as if it is a fact) that *Jeremy Corbyn is unelectable* or, in the case of the recent US Presidential Election, that *Mrs Clinton is a criminal,* or that *all immigrants are terrorists. Truthiness* is surely the final barbarism. Unless we can disown it altogether, we shall have lost not just an important function of the English language, but an important part of our civilisation.

[1] *Encore,* July 2005.
[2] *Op cit,* August 2005.
[3] See Brian Freeland, *Around the World in Eighty Plays,* ATWP, 2015. p.155.

4

GOING FORWARD

Clutching a little case
He walks out briskly to infect a city
Whose terrible future may have just arrived.

W. H. Auden, Gare du Midi.

America is not the most taxed country on earth, nor is climate change a Chinese hoax. Yet thanks to the low standard of much mainline news, millions believed both.

The Times, Editorial, 15 November, 2016.

In November 2016 the *Oxford English Dictionary* announced that 'post-truth' was its 'Word of the Year 2016'. It defined the term as 'relating to or denoting circumstances in which objective facts are less influential in shaping public opinion than appeals to emotion and personal belief'. Among the runners-up were 'Adulting' (the practice of behaving in a way characteristic of a responsible adult), Chatbot (a computer programme designed to stimulate conversation over the

internet with human users) and Coulrophobia (Extreme fear of clowns). The words were not chosen because they were already widely used (obviously) but chosen to 'reflect the social, cultural, political, economic and technological trends and events' that had characterised the Referendum and after.

So the *Oxford English Dictionary* felt able to say without apology that we were, post-Referendum, living in a 'Post-Truth Age'. At another time we might have bridled at the description, and asserted that we still relied upon those sources of 'news' that we knew to be truthful – the B.B.C., Sky News, *The Times*, or *The Morning Star*, according to choice – adding that we were not easily fooled and could still distinguish truth from falsity, thank you very much. And of course there are still people like that, but the majority now rely on gaining their 'latest information' from the *Electronic Reality* of their smartpads and i-phones – a sure sign that we are indeed lost in a 'Post-Truth Age', for in these shadowy realms lies grow like poisonous weeds.

Consider the following 'news items', all *trending*

throughout the period of the 2016 presidential election in the US. Each of them contained an element of 'truthiness' (i.e. *felt* as if they ought to be true) – but which of them was based on 'objective fact'?:

  ◆ The Pope has endorsed Donald Trump's candidacy.
  ◆ Michelle Obama is urging the closure of all museums because they only serve white people.
  ◆ After the Inauguration Mrs Clinton will be given a Free Pardon for her crimes.
  ◆ Bill Clinton's Sex Tapes have just been released to the press.

Of course they are all lies, but at the time they were read by tens of thousands of people, and their 'truthiness' meant they were believed, at least by some. Nor is this solely an American problem. In the UK media analysts say that some thirty per cent of 'news' stories on Twitter are untrue.

But at least followers of social media could take comfort from the fact that what was trending, whether truth or fantasy, surely reflected the genuine *voice of the people*? Then even that solace was removed from them. Analysis of Facebook's content revealed that it was not the approval of the population which caused certain stories to trend, but an algorithm which chose them solely for their market impact – that is, for their likely popularity, and their truthiness. Such algorithms are designed to identify and exploit mass markets. They make no distinction between selling their users a new washing powder, and selling them an attractive political slogan.[1] So media-savvy politicians now have direct access to the same emotional 'triggers' that sell us our tee shirts, our trainers and our energy giving drinks.

Public Opinion

Throughout the eighteenth and nineteenth centuries there were intermittent attempts in the US to gauge 'public opinion' by means of polling sample groups. But the practice did not become systematised until the work of George Gallup in the 1930s.[2] The technique was not used to any significant effect in the UK until after the Second World War, and even then public opinion polls operated at a primitive level. They forecast that Winston Churchill would easily win the first post-war election (whereas in fact Clement Attlee's Labour Party won in a landslide). Thereafter, with more sophisticated polling techniques, the pollsters have enjoyed more success, until recent years when forecasts of the way elections might go in the UK, in mainland Europe and in the USA have often been embarrassingly wide of the mark. This has led some pollsters to cover all bases by using the sort of bets-hedging language favoured by Mystic Meg and her fellows: *You are heading for a fateful encounter – which could go either way...*

As we have already suggested, it seems that some people's 'opinions' are now shaped by the algorithms of Facebook, rather than by any class allegiance or by disinterested consideration of political policies. As a result some pollsters have started to ask not 'Who are you voting for?' but rather, 'What are you voting *against*?' Popular modern politicians do not offer *aspirations*, but plausible scapegoats, set up so they can be blamed for every ill. Even if the scapegoat is something as nebulous as *The Brussels Bureaucrats*, it is still something which in the world of *Electronic Reality* can be held responsible for every irritation – from those dratted *Health and Safety Regulations* through the price of beer to the (alleged) forbidding of the sale of bent bananas.

Studies of the way opinions are formed[3] point to the fact that conversions to a new cause will often be near-instantaneous (sometimes described as 'seeing the light' or 'a light bulb moment'). When describing their conversion – to Marxism, Buddhism or Teetotalism, say – a subject will characteristically tell of a period of despair and inner turmoil followed by a sudden gestalt, a blinding flash, like Saul on the road to Damascus, which in an instant converted them. Yet during the 2016 Referendum campaign there seemed to be few if any 'light bulb moments'. People were converted to the Bremain or the Brexit cause by lengthier and less showy means. So, something else was at work there.

Some hint of its nature may be found in the work of Mary Aiken, a 'cyberpsychologist', who explains her new field of interest thus;

> I study human interactions with technology and digital media, mobile and networked devices, gaming, virtual reality, artificial intelligence (AI) and intelligence amplification (IA) – anything from cellphones to cyborgs. But mostly I concentrate on internet psychology. If anything qualifies as "technology" and has the potential to affect or change human behaviour, I want to look at how – and consider why.[4]

In Electronic Reality – more than half the population now gets some or all of its 'news' from the social media – people are fast losing whatever ability they may once have had to separate truth from lies. As Dr Aiken warns us:

> Many people deny the awareness that they have entered
> a new dimension when they go Online… They are sitting
> in their own homes, surrounded by familiar objects, and
> their bodies are resting in the cushions of familiar chairs
> and sofas. In their minds they have not "gone" anywhere.
> But the conditions and qualities of the online environment
> are different from real life. That is why our instincts, which
> have evolved to handle face-to-face interactions, fail us in
> cyberspace.

In the 'post-truth' world of cyberspace, with its never-
ending supply of 'truthiness' and over-simplified 'news',
people lose their former bearings. They newly inhabit a
misty realm full of suspicions – that there is a plot to foil the
Brexiteers and to allow Bremainers to triumph, that this or that
country is out to destroy the City of London, NATO or British
farmers, that a second referendum is being secretly planned
– or that the authorities are conspiring in other devious ways
to do them harm. Fragments of politicians' speeches will be
daily seized upon, as evidence of these malign conspiracies.
A memorandum carried by a parliamentary messenger out
of 10 Downing Street and photographed by the prowling
paparazzi (29.11.2016), headed 'Having your cake and
eating it' was made much of, as was the email sent to his staff
(2.1.2017) by Sir Ivan Rogers, the UK's Ambassador to the
European Union, at the time of his unexpected resignation.
    But let's stop pussyfooting around and instead, to
employ another piece of useful slang, *let's cut the PM some
slack*. Let us assume that she and her advisers are perfectly

well aware that you can't have your cake and eat it – that she already knows it is impossible both to remain fully in the EU free market *and* disallow free movement of labour, that she also knows it is impossible to 'take back' the UK legal system and retain the 'passporting' arrangements which allow European businesses to operate from London. And, as she is also an experienced politician, let us also assume that she will not wish to alienate large numbers of voters by any incautious use of language. She will be as bland and noncommittal as she can.

Bearing all that in mind, suppose – just suppose – that **Mrs May does not herself particularly care** *about the precise meaning of 'Brexit means Brexit'.* And just suppose (and we apologise for the indelicacy of the mental picture this invokes), just suppose for the sake of argument that Mrs May's infamous phrase *Brexit means Brexit* was a verbal fig leaf beneath which she could enjoy a little more wriggle room, as she prepared to negotiate with the EU.

Mrs May needed, and still needs, all the *wriggle room* she can get. Whatever legerdemain she and her negotiators may adopt, and whatever slick redefinitions they may employ to package their results, the fact of the matter is that the UK negotiators cannot avoid these awkward truths, 1) Non EU members will not ever be given open and unlimited access to the Single Market, and 2) While the UK remains a member of the EU, it cannot impose blanket restrictions on immigration – certainly not of the kind that will bring immigration down to 'the tens of thousands', as Mrs May has pledged. Whatever our negotiating aims may have been, in these and in all other areas, there will have to be compromise.

So when the hubbub finally dies down, in two, three or ten years' time, *Brexit* will be seen to consist of a jumbled pile of wriggling prevarications, murmuring objectors and tiny, lifeless compromises. It will be a permanent eyesore – not hard enough for some, too soft for others, too like Bremain for the agitators on one side, and too like total capitulation for the zealots on the other. Yet the term will take its place in the pantheon of UK history, and students as yet unborn will write learned dissertations about it, speculating whether something which was simultaneously so ill-understood and yet so massively disruptive was born of real historical necessity, or was merely the consequence of vainglorious political posturing on behalf of a handful of our political leaders.

[1] It transpired that some of the 'fake news' during the US presidential election was transmitted or re-transmitted by computer literate youths in Macedonia.

[2] See George Gallup, *Public Opinion in a Democracy*, New York, USA, 1939

[3] See Jacob and Michal Shamir, *The Anatomy of Public Opinion*, University of Michigan Press, USA, 2,000

[4] See Mary Aiken, *The Cyber Effect; A Pioneering Cyberpsychologist Explains How Human Behaviour Changes Online*, Murray, 2016.

5

THINGS BEING VARIOUS

How many more bloody awful words was this ghastly mess going to throw up? Did the English language have to die along with Britain's ties to the European Union?

'Enid Blyton' (Bruno Vincent), *Five on Brexit Island,* **2017.**

The use of cyberspace to promote radicalisation and terrorism is among the greatest problems faced by Britain and other western Countries. Networks such as Facebook, Twitter and YouTube are the vehicle of choice in spreading propaganda and recruiting platforms for terrorism.

Commons Home Affairs Selection Committee, 24 August, 2016.

40 states now have some cyber military capabilities, 12 of them for aggressive cyberwarfare.

UN Report, 2017.

There cannot, in all political history, ever have been a less appropriate term than the announcement that in early 2017 Mrs May would *trigger* the opening of negotiations between the UK and the EU. *Trigger?* Does a priest *trigger* Evensong? Does the Queen *trigger* the Opening of Parliament? The opening of these curious conversations was surely a matter of political etiquette, not an act of aggression. In any case the EU Countries already knew the result of the UK Referendum, and already knew the date on which the negotiations would begin, and the ensuing months and years would be more like a long board game than the sort of contest opened by pulling the trigger on a starter gun. If the EU negotiations have to be thought of as some sort of a duel it will surely be an unusually protracted one, and fought with something less murderous than pistols. As its opening was formally signalled, it should perhaps have been pictured as a lady dropping a dainty handkerchief.

In the crumbs of comfort she occasionally offers the UK electorate Mrs May portrays herself as a sturdy traditionalist. In a recent interview she revealed that one of her girlish heroines was the bob-haired Emma Peel, the glamorous karate expert from *The Avengers* and, dipping deeper into her nostalgia bag (though still exhibiting a disdain for concrete language) confided that she wanted a *Red, White and Blue Brexit*. That didn't take us very far. It merely gave her a slightly broader fig leaf: *Red, White and Blue Brexit means Red, White and Blue Brexit means leaving the EU.* More wriggle room?

Putting that image once more from our minds, let us look at the terms in which these negotiations are being conducted, set out (p.1-2 *above*) in Article 50 of the EU

Lisbon Treaty. This document says that negotiations will *normally* take two years, adding the significant rider, *unless the European Council, in agreement with the Member State, agrees to extend this period.* So, if there is agreement on both sides, negotiations between the EU and the UK can, in whole or part, continue beyond 2019. *And there is no time limit put upon this period of extended negotiation.* It could, as the UK's former Ambassador to the EU is said to have warned the Cabinet, take up to ten years. And, at least in theory, it could last for the length of time other international negotiations – Israel's border disputes with Palestine, say, or the reunification of Crete – have so far taken.

Moreover, further examination of Article 50 shows that leaving the EU is not an irrevocable act. See Article 50, Note 5; If a State has withdrawn from the EU and wishes to rejoin, its request shall be subject to the procedure referred to in Article 49. So one turns with fluttering heart to Article 49, wondering what chasms must be bridged and what obstacles overcome before 'rejoining' can even be considered. Only to find that it seems comparatively easy. Here is Article 49, reproduced in its entirety:

Article 49

Any European State which respects the values referred to in Article 2, and is committed to promoting them may apply to become a member of the Union. The European Parliament and National Parliaments shall be notified of the application. The applicant State shall address its application to the Council, which shall act unanimously after consulting the Commission and after receiving the assent of the European Parliament, which shall act by an absolute majority of its component members. He conditions of admission and the adjustment of the Treaties on which the Union is formed, which such admission entails, shall be the subject of an agreement between the member states and the applicant state. The agreement shall be submitted for ratification by all the contracting states in accordance with their respective constitutional requirements. The conditions of eligibility agreed upon by the European Council shall be taken into account.

Anyone with any knowledge of contract law will see readily enough that an applicant who finds favour with the EU hierarchy could, with their assistance, *drive a coach and horses through* terms as loosely phrased as these. Equally there is plenty of scope, in the case of an unwanted application, for the EU mandarins just to *kick it into the long grass.* So, just supposing the UK had negotiated terms on which to leave the EU, but the population at large or (a new?) Parliament disliked them, the UK *could*, with the agreement of one and all, annul their departure and open negotiations to rejoin. We would have the great advantage that we already *knew the ropes.* We *might* even be welcomed back. As a fairly wealthy nation, already inward with EU regulations and the ways of the Brussels bureaucrats, we *might* in those circumstances even stand a chance of regaining our former position relative to our European partners.

Dream on. Of course it is difficult, if not impossible, to conceive of European governments being charitably disposed to a former EU member that has recently caused them such disquiet. Yet these apparent loopholes are worth bearing in mind, not least because we are after all the first country ever to leave the EU and the laws governing departure have been loosely framed. There are other intangibles. Either of the two parties to the discussions might over the next few years radically change its nature. Resignations, assassinations, unexpected election results, financial collapses, impeachments, new cyber wars – all kinds of events could radically alter the course of the negotiations. And, lurking on the sidelines, the rise across Europe of that strange new anti-political force commentators call *populism.*

And, even if circumstances do not radically change, we must not assume that the UK and the 27 remaining members of the EU will necessarily find compromises to agree upon. After all, it only takes the parliament of one of the EU states to refuse to accept the negotiated terms, for it all – at least in theory – to be rendered null and void. Indeed, the more we look into the matter, the more we may conclude that what we did together on June 23rd 2016, far from being *the most important decision we would make in our lifetimes*, was not really decisive at all. It has led to a bureaucratic jamboree that is at least as labyrinthine and expensive as anything dreamed up by the EU bureaucracy, a jamboree from which we, the ordinary voters, are rigidly excluded. Indeed we, the *people* whose *voice* was not so very long ago thought to be decisive, are left to look silently on, comforted only by the knowledge that we have given the European political Wonderland a new term.

'Twas Brexit...

Lewis Carroll's nightmare visions seem to be a useful metaphor for recording the processes of EU withdrawal. The actions of the thirty thousand civil servants employed in plotting the UK's path through these labyrinthine negotiations recall the purblind rituals of the voyagers in *The Hunting of the Snark*. When Mrs May, in an uncharacteristic slip of the tongue, told a BBC interviewer (2.1.2017) that she would be sitting *around* the table with EU negotiators, it was inevitable that the Mad Hatter's tea party, at which guests constantly moved around the table, should come to mind. And we must always bear in mind the vainglorious heroics of *Jabberwocky*: *'Twas Brillig, and the slithy toves/did gyre and gimble in the wabe...'*

Although we might find depictions of the same surreal, inverted world elsewhere in literature:

> The room was suddenly rich and the great bay-window was
> Spawning snow and pink roses against it

Soundlessly collateral and incompatible:
World is suddener than we fancy it.

World is crazier and more of it than we think,
Incorrigibly plural. I peel a grape and portion
A tangerine and spit the pips and feel
The drunkenness of things being various.[1]

Other writers – Ionesco, Swift perhaps, or even Kafka – come to mind. Each in his different way catches something of the nightmarish fantasy of the *Brexit* years, but nothing of its underlying turgidity. To depict this side of things we must turn to a writer with a dull civil service mind, a chronicler of the humdrum and the mundane. So finally we conclude that the *Brexit* years, more than anything, resemble an adventure story jointly written by Lewis Carroll and C. P. Snow.

The intelligence we receive of the negotiations' progress does not of course aspire to such fanciful heights. Instead events, unimportant though they may often be, are couched in the familiar media jargon of *alliances, power blocs, barriers, bombshells countdowns, crises and confrontations.* Even when there is nothing of substance to report, headlines have still to be fabricated, gossip repeated and rumour spread. Our politicians, while keeping their negotiating positions secret will, as the inevitable compromises are revealed, go on telling us, with eyes open wide as saucers, that they have always been *very clear* or even *very, very clear* about the fact that they are trying to achieve *what's **good** for this country* and ***right** for Britain.* (Whatever that may be.)

So how are we to survive this verbal onslaught? How are we to stay sane through the coming months, years or decades when we already feel like projectile vomiting each time we hear the word *Brexit*, and are already bored to distraction by arguments over *precedence, polarity* or *priority*? How can we escape the verbal battering which threatens to engulf us?

Emigration to a desert island, though tempting, is not unfortunately an option. Nor can we, as we go about our daily business, seek totally to ignore the politicians' spin, and the daily switchback ride, lurching violently from wild optimism to sudden despair, on which the media would like to take us. But we do not have to be manipulated by this army of malevolent wordsmiths. We can instead protect ourselves with a mindful device that filters and corrects the distortions in what we are being told. At the same time each of us can try to cultivate an inner serenity, reminding ourselves that we are part of a natural world infinitely greater than the raucous hysteria of *Brexit*, secure in the knowledge that the sun will continue to rise and set, the leaves will still bud and fall and the oceans ebb and flow, disdaining all the *confrontations, crises, battles* and *bureaucratic bluster* of the seemingly endless EU negotiations.

In a word we need to recapture an inward calm, which prevents the clamour of *Electronic Reality* from rising to torment us:

All things on the move, going their own little ways, and all
Jostling, people touching and talking and making small
Contacts and bouncing off again, bounce! bounce like a ball!

My flesh is weary with bounce and gone again! –
My ears are weary with words that bounce on them and then
Bounce off again, meaning nothing. Assertions! Assertions!

Stones, women and men![2]

Unmoved by the brickbats of arrogant commentators, believing that our collective decision to leave the EU may have been the single *most important* decision that would be made in our *politicians' lifetimes* but not in ours, and unmoved by the predictions of self-serving bureaucrats, we must all go on living our lives in as measured a fashion as possible. In moments of tranquility we can amuse ourselves by imagining that the 2016 Referendum had never been called, and speculate upon what momentous questions the 30.000 well-paid UK bureaucrats now involved in the EU negotiations might have been engaged in resolving, if *Brexit* had never been heard of.

But the Referendum did take place and *Brexit* was fashioned from its ruins. We now find ourselves spectators at an extended post-apocalyptic conference, a bureaucratic exchange to which we ordinary voters are denied admittance. Its eventual outcomes may be of some importance to some of us – though of less significance than much else that shapes our lives – but meanwhile our only involvement is to help foot the bill. So we must stand back, count our daily blessings and try to close our ears to the commands and complaints of those whose paid business it is to convince us that their convoluted nostrums matter more than our trivial round and common task.

More than ever, the price of being fully alive is eternal vigilance. In that daily struggle the following rules may help:

1) Never accept political terms – meaning almost all of the words and phrases italicised in this book – at their face

value. In the 1950s the philosopher Stebbing [Note to PC hounds, she *liked* to be addressed by her surname] suggested that arguments about the morality of war would be clarified if, every time we used the word 'war', we substituted some such phrase as 'the indiscriminate killing of men, women and children'. In the same way we must get into the habit of substituting, for duplicitous political words and phrases, what is *really* meant – for example, *Post Truth* means *lying*. We must in particular watch out for those words (*immigration, transference, tariff*) whose meanings are at present being subtly expanded or contracted to meet the shoddy purposes of a forthcoming bureaucratic compromise.

2. Be wary of false dichotomies, even apparently harmless ones such as the politicians' distinction between '*our friends*' and '*our enemies*'. Divisions such as this are invariably transient in nature. This particular one can lead us into making alliances with brutal tyrants, and ignoring the vulnerable and needy.

3. Always suspect political generalisations – including those in this book – and especially those making use of racial or gender stereotypes.

4. When considering political arguments, now or in the future, be on the lookout for hidden premises – such as the half-buried assumption that working class people are poor because they are feckless and stupid, or that the need to make profits from the arms industry naturally overrides any humanitarian concern. A surfeit of such hidden premises will gradually dull our ability to make luminous moral

distinctions and leave us reacting, like lab rats, only to the crudest of stimuli.

5. Do not allow others to dictate the terms of debate. (3) Leaving, or remaining in, the EU for example involves questions of language, loyalty, culture, nationhood, religion and tradition in addition to the dictates of economics and material wealth that so concern our politicians.

6. When the inevitable compromises with the EU are eventually reached, beware any heroic posturing on the part of the UK negotiators. By their very nature, outcomes which are proclaimed to be '**good** *for Britain*' must *also* be '**good**' for each of the 27 European countries whose Parliaments will have to ratify them. And after all we didn't expect them to blazon forth the news that they had negotiated outcomes that were **bad** for Britain, now did we?

Finally, though wishing our readers well, we call down an authors' curse on all those who, from ignorance, greed or malice, are attempting to twist the *Brexit* negotiations to suit their own political ends. May they be fittingly dispatched.

[1] Louis MacNiece, Snow.
[2] D. H. Lawrence, Song of a Man Who is Loved.
[3] See George Lakoff, Don't Think of an Elephant, Chelsea Green, USA, 2004, p.3.

A SHORT GLOSSARY
OF POLITICAL FLANNEL

Anyone habitually using more than three of these terms in political argument can safely be accounted a knave or a fool.

Abbreviations *v.b.* Verbal bluster, useful for disguising the fact you don't know what you are talking about, but don't want anybody else to speak, just in case they do. *A*.indicates that the word has diametrically opposed meanings.

academic Common, sneer meaning. 'Probably true but only someone who has spent the last fifty years blindfolded in a Tibetan Monastery could possibly think it applies in this case.' *A.* Scrupulously argued and highly relevant.

appropriate That which the speaker approves of.

aspirational Utopian. Best avoided, as it implies straining for ridiculously over-ambitious goals that cannot be reached in the lifetime of one Parliament.

At this moment in time *v.b.* Now.

A very good question Stalling for time by congratulating the interviewer. [Also] I'm really glad you asked me that.

bank A well-established financial institution which in normal times relies for its regular income on keeping its clients in permanent debt. In abnormal times it will be bailed out by taxpayers as an essential tool in national economic growth. Its leaders are traditionally paid massive salaries, which arouses envious comment from its debtors.

benefits Freebies (such as housing, cars, colour television, priority in NHS treatment, free clothing) which are, as everybody knows, handed out to all immigrants as soon as they step off the boat. *A.* 'Quite right too!' or 'Its got to stop!'

bombshell An event that has not been correctly predicted by politicians. *Plural:* whammy.

Bremainer One who gormlessly refuses to accept the outcome of the 2016 Referendum, on the grounds that all those who voted for Brexit had the brains of an ink monitor and the morals of a lettuce. *A.* A wise statesman who has the good of his country at heart.

Brexiteer A reckless adventurer; one who gives no thought to his children's futures and would happily sell his grandchildren into slavery. *A.* A wise statesman who has the good of his country at heart.

bribe Essential means of concluding business deals with Johnny Foreigner. (*see b*ung)

buggery (From breakfast to) An imaginary destination to which a businessman might aspire to kick a rival, or the same place to which a rival might want to kick him.

Bull Market A delicate poetic allusion to the way profits are serviced, and one's rivals shafted.

bung Traditionally delivered in a brown envelope, a reward for closing a deal with Johnny Foreigner or for keeping shtum over that little business in Qatar. (*see* bribe)

businessmen A fine upstanding group of patriots who exist to serve their country with never a thought for themselves. (*see* bung)

caring All-purpose word used to describe any action or group about which you want the voters to feel positive. (*see c*ommunity)

community All-purpose word used to describe any group or action about which you want the voters to feel positive. (*See c*aring)

confronting (terrorism, the national debt, etc.) *v.b.* Strong and lusty verb useful for hiding the fact that you are scared stiff of something or that you haven't the remotest idea what to do about it.

dead in the water Descriptive of any useful idea a political opponent may have had.

determined *v.b.* Used to give emphasis to unconvincing PR, e.g. 'The PM is determined to make this her number one priority (*q.v.*)'

dither What your opponent does – in contrast to your side which of course takes time to come to a measured decision.

drawing the short straw Plagued with bad luck – according to you.

egg on your face (left with) Metaphorical allusion to the result of drawing the short straw. (*q.v.*)

First, I'd just like to say... *v.b.* Well-known distraction when a politician does not wish to answer.

Frankly speaking... *v.b.* A traditional precursor to a blatant political lie.

going forward v.b. The Holy Grail of political flannel. A perfectly meaningless term, which can be used at any time, but which always sounds vaguely purposeful.

good (for trade, Britain, the City etc.) *v.b.* Suits my book.

hard-working (people, families etc) Reluctance to use the old Marxist term 'working class' but equally patronising, and equally false, carrying the implication that the unemployed would all prefer to stay that way.

harking back to the past Care is needed here as it can be used as a term of abuse; 'My opponent wants to hark back to the past', or to remind people helpfully of how smart you are by comparison: 'In their fourteen years in power the party opposite did nothing about this problem.'

move on (time to) Sweep it all under the carpet.

next level (take it to the) Somewhere to which you are not allowed access.

nitty gritty (Let's get down to the) Let's talk on my terms.

number one priority (It's our) *v.b.* Phrase used to silence those who accuse you of dragging your feet.

ordinary voters (the majority of) The minority that agrees with me.

populism/populist *A.* A term which can either be applied sneeringly to a popular left-wing group or to the shifty

technique by which a right-wing extremist tricks his or her way into power.

short term *A.* A quick fix pending a long-term solution or The long-term solution itself.

The fact of the matter is... *v.b.* Another well-known precursor of a bare-faced political lie.

The jury's out on this one. *v.b.* I have not yet been told what to think by my party's managers.

To speak plainly... *v.b.* Watch out! I'm brewing up another whopper.

quantitative easing Printing money.

We still have work to do. *v.b.* See The jury's out on this one.

Where we are today. The mess we've got you in.

will of the people An unknowable entity invoked by the speaker to bolster his/her argument.

win-win (situation) An impracticability, otherwise Brexit and Bremain could have been equally satisfactory in outcome and there would have been no point in holding the ruddy Referendum.

zero-hours contract One of those many things – like train delays or rough sleepers – that ordinary people have daily experience of, but which are invisible to most politicians.

DEEPER READING

Kingsley Amis, *The King's English*, US, St. Martin's Press, 1997.

Bruce Fraser, revised version of Sir Ernest Gower's *Complete Plain Words*, HMSO, 1973.

John Humphrys, *Lost for Words: The Mangling and Manipulation of The English Language*, Hodder and Stoughton, 2004.

John Humphrys, *Beyond Language: How Language Reveals The Way We Live Now*, Hodder and Stoughton, 2006.

Ian Robinson, *The Survival of English*, Brynmill, 1980.

Keith Waterhouse, *Waterhouse on Newspaper Style*, Penguin, 1993.

69780897R00058

Made in the USA
Columbia, SC
22 April 2017